When THE WORD Comes Alive

AN OVERVIEW OF JOHN

JACK HAYFORD
SCOTT BAUER • JACK HAMILTON

WHEN WORD COMES ALIVE
A Practical, Introductory Guidebook for a
Comprehensive Overview in the Bible Book of
JOHN

Unless otherwise noted, all Scripture references are from the
New King James Version:
Copyright © 1979, 1980, 1982 by Thomas Nelson, Inc.,
Nashville, Tennessee.
Maps and illustrations taken from the *Nelson's Complete Book of
Bible Maps and Charts*, ©1993, Thomas Nelson, Inc. Used by
permission.
Outline of Acts taken from the *Spirit-Filled Life Bible*, ©1991,
Thomas Nelson, Inc. Used by permission.

Photographs of Dr. Jack Hayford, Dr. Scott Bauer, and
Dr. Jack Hamilton by Christopher Glenn Photography.

Published by Living Way Ministries
14300 Sherman Way
Van Nuys, CA (USA) 91405-2499
(818) 779-8400 • (800) 776-8180

ISBN 0-916847-20-9
Printed in the United States of America

TABLE OF CONTENTS

GROWING WITH THE BIBLE BOOK-A-MONTH STUDIES

Disciples of the Lord Jesus Christ know it: *There is no substitute for the Word of God in our daily lives!* Still, many find that the formation of a satisfying, fulfilling discipline in reading and studying God's Word is not easy. In contrast, many fall into a merely regimented or legalistic habit that eventually withers for lack of the Holy Spirit's breath upon it. Others have difficulty finding direction or maintaining focus; besides, we all need help to keep us moving forward *through* the Word.

The formulation of the "Bible Book-A-Month" concept was born in the heart of Dr. Jack Hayford, who, as a pastor, constantly seeks improved means of helping people achieve three things: *systematic, substantial,* and *thorough* coverage of the Bible. Each is important to accomplish the objective of good Bible study, and they can be realized through this plan.

(1) It's <u>systematic</u>, by reason of the *month-by-month* advancement of the program; (2) it's <u>substantial</u>, because of the *spiritual weight* of the triangular

approach of study employed; and (3) it's <u>thorough</u>, for *every book* of the Bible is incorporated in it.

THE TRIANGULAR APPROACH

There are many worthwhile approaches to a study of the Holy Bible. For example, "synthetic" study—which draws together highlights to provide a quick grasp of a book; "critical" study—which assesses the ancient textual resources that authenticate the trustworthiness of the book as a document; or "verse-by-verse" study—which seeks to exhaust every book of the totality of its content.

Distinct from any of these, the "Bible Book-A-Month" study seeks to achieve the maximum possible grasp of a book's truth while keeping a pace forward which sustains the average Bible student's interest. It is <u>demanding</u> enough in its *academics* to seriously engage those interested in intelligent, thought-provoking study. Yet it is <u>dynamic</u> enough in its *movement* to avoid losing passion, and to keep each student at a point of continuous anticipation. This is done through use of a **"triangular approach"** to each book—which focuses the three primary things to be found in every book of the Bible.

1. Each Bible book contains an *essential message*: the core concepts which distinguish that book and provide its place in God's Word. This is found in *towering truths* and *pillar passages* within that book. These together provide a rich overview of the Holy Spirit's theme and thrust in that book of the Bible.

2. Each Bible book presents *problems* and evokes *questions* rising from the need to integrate that book's content with the whole Bible, as well as to interpret its content as it addresses current issues. Good Bible study helps questioners find *satisfactory answers* to reasoned inquiry, even as it demonstrates the *relevancy* of God's Word to today's social problems. Thus, we discover the power of the Holy Spirit—present to reveal Christ to the world—TODAY!

3. Each Bible book provides *practical wisdom* and *personal guidance*; it sheds light on the believer's daily walk and service as he or she follows Jesus Christ. Healthy study in God's Word should provide *information* and *inspiration*, but only as it issues in *incarnation* does it achieve its goal! In each book, *insights for faithful, fruitful pathways* will show how to adopt, adapt, and apply the Bible to your life, as Jesus' disciple.

These perspectives provide the viewpoints which "triangulate" on the text: each book studied through three lessons which unfold the truth of God's Word noting one of the above three values. The "Bible Book-A-Month" triangular approach works this way:

• Dr. Jack Hayford's presentation is first, providing a full picture of the purpose and message of each book.

• Dr. Scott Bauer's lesson is second, affording a grasp of the relevancy of each book and revealing the Spirit's power as it unveils Jesus Himself.

- Dr. Jack Hamilton's lesson is third in each volume, presenting the practical lessons of each book.

By means of these three lessons, a comprehensive overview of a book (or books) of the Bible is presented in each study, so it can be truly gained, grasped, and applied.

TRIPLE TOOLS—SUPPORT RESOURCES

1. Each study is accented by a *pocket-sized book* approximately 72 pages long. Each book presents focused analyses by Drs. Hayford, Bauer, and Hamilton on one or more books of the Bible.

2. Pastor Hayford has been asked by a national distributor of audio Bibles to record the whole Bible in the New King James Version. These *audio books of the Bible* are being produced now, and each reading can be ordered in conjunction with the ***Bible Book-A-Month*** program.

3. Each lesson in the monthly teaching series is available on audio cassette for further review and study. The *teaching tapes* and readings of the Bible join with the printed books to complete the support resources for the ***Bible Book-A-Month*** studies.

Additional resources, noted in each volume, can also be ordered by calling Living Way Ministries at 818-779-8480 or 800-776-8180.

JOHN:
THE KEY WORD IS "BELIEVE."

The fourth gospel has the clearest statement of purpose in the Bible: "But these are written that you may believe that Jesus is the Christ, the Son of God, and that believing you may have life in His name" (20:31). John selected the signs he used for the specific purpose of creating intellectual and spiritual conviction about the Son of God.

KEY VERSES

"He came to His own, and His own did not receive Him. But as many as received Him, to them He gave the right to become children of God, to those who believe in His name: who were born, not of blood, nor of the will of the flesh, nor of the will of man, but of God."
John 1:11-13

"And truly Jesus did many other signs in the presence of His disciples, which are not written in this book; but these are written that you may believe that Jesus is the Christ, the Son of God, and that believing you may have life in His name." John 20:30-31

KEY CHAPTER: JOHN 3

John 3:16 is without doubt the most quoted and preached verse in all of Scripture. Captured in it is the gospel in its clearest and simplest form: that salvation is a gift of God and is obtainable only through belief.

Introducing the Bible Book of
JOHN

Author:	The Apostle John
Date:	About A.D. 85
Theme:	Knowing God by Believing in Jesus Christ
Key Words:	Believe, Bear Witness, Life

AUTHOR

Early church tradition attributes the Fourth Gospel to John "the beloved disciple" (13:23; 19:26; 20:2; 21:7, 20), who belonged to the "inner circle" of Jesus' followers (see Matthew 17:1; Mark 13:3). According to Christian writers of the second century, John moved to Ephesus, probably during the Jewish War of A.D. 66-70, where he continued his ministry.

Some scholars suggest that John 19:35 and 21:24 may reflect another author who faithfully collected the eyewitness account and testimonials. However, the bulk of the evidence, both internal and external, supports John the apostle as the author.

DATE

The same tradition that locates John in Ephesus suggests that he wrote his Gospel in the latter part of the first century. In the absence of substantial evidence to the contrary, most scholars accept this tradition.

PERIOD IN WHICH
JOHN WAS LIKELY WRITTEN

BIRTH OF JESUS 4 B.C.	ASCENSION OF JESUS PENTECOST A.D. 30	COUNCIL OF JERUSALEM A.D. 49	PERSECUTION BY NERO A.D. 64-68	DEATH OF JOHN C.A.D. 100
			DESTRUCTION OF TEMPLE A.D. 70	

John displays Jesus as God's Son, verified by signs that point to faith, commitment, and service.

PART 1

THE
PILLAR
PRINCIPLES
OF
JOHN

JACK HAYFORD

THE "I AM" STATEMENTS

Twenty-three times in all we find our Lord's meaningful "I AM" (*ego eimi*, Gk.) in the Greek text of this Gospel (4:26; 6:20, 35, 41, 48, 51; 8:12, 18, 24, 28, 58; 10:7, 9, 11, 14; 11:25; 13:19; 14:6; 15:1, 5; 18:5, 6, 8). In several of these He joins His "I AM" with seven tremendous metaphors which are expressive of His saving relationship toward the world.

"I AM the Bread of life" (6:35, 41, 48, 51).

"I AM the Light of the world" (8:12).

"I AM the Door of the sheep" (10:7, 9).

"I AM the Good Shepherd" (10:11, 14).

"I AM the Resurrection and the Life" (11:25).

"I AM the Way, the Truth, the Life" (14:6).

"I AM the true Vine" (15:1, 5).

THE PILLAR PRINCIPLES OF
JOHN

John's Gospel has been called "the most profound book in the world," while at the same time is used as the *first* book most young believers in Christ are given as they initiate their walk with the Savior.

This remarkable fact—that the same book is at once the "most profound" and the most simply understood—illustrates the glory and grandeur of this Gospel, which begins by telling us that *time and eternity have met in the Person of Jesus!*

"When The Word Comes Alive" has been titled in the conviction that what God did in Christ He is still seeking to do through the Church by the Holy Spirit's power. In short, the incarnation of the Second Person of the Godhead—*The Son*—was not only to <u>complete</u> the provision of Redemption's Plan, but to <u>commence</u> the advance of the Redeemer's Church. *Both* involve *incarnation*—that is, bringing God's Word *into human flesh* that It might be transmitted *unto humankind.*

John 1:14 is the fountainhead text of this truth: *"And the Word became flesh and dwelt among us, and we beheld His glory, the glory as of the only begotten of the Father, full of grace and truth."*

Two great things happened when the Word <u>CAME</u> alive:

(1) The <u>purpose</u> of this heavenly incarnation is to "dwell" with humankind—not simply "pass by," but to "live among, to be with." Thus, God became human not simply to make an <u>appearance</u> to impress us, but to spend a <u>lifetime</u> so none could ever say, "He doesn't understand what my life is like."

(2) The <u>presentation</u> made through the incarnation was glorious—that is, excelling in its beauty and blessing—being filled with *grace* and *truth*. Foremost in significance is the order—"grace" is first, with "truth" coming *after* people were able to see the breadth of the gentle love and welcoming acceptance God showed humankind.

The double features in this display of God's "style" in "*so loving the world*" are insight-filled for each of us who would say, "Jesus, *now come alive* through me just as You lived before." Of course, this is exactly what He has declared His desired plan to be. He said, "As the Father sent Me, so I am sending you!" (John 20:20), and "The works that I do shall (you) also do!" (John 14:12). Heaven's objective is clear: the plan is to *save* sinners, then *send* saints—*the Redeemed are recovered to become empowered agents who relay the same grace, love, and power that the Redeemer revealed.*

So, it is with this baseline of understanding that we open the Gospel of John. We want to see "what happens when the Word of God *comes alive.*" We not only want to know what happened then, when

God <u>lived</u> His life in human form, but what can happen today when people like us whom He's rescued recognize how much He still "so loves" the world, and will let Him *love through us* as well as live in us. This approach makes our pursuit of John more than merely academic—we are aimed for *action*, beginning with a commitment to allow the Holy Spirit to (1) <u>light</u> our hearts and minds as we see Jesus in this Gospel, then (2) <u>ignite</u> our whole being in such a way that our bodies become vehicles which incarnate heaven's grace and truth, just as He did!

(Exercise: To apply this idea, go back and think through the "two great concepts" mentioned, which are seen in Jesus' incarnation—purpose and presentation. Take time to write out how these features, seen in Christ's coming to show the Father to us, point the way for you and me toward a clearer understanding of how we can be redemptive agents in the life-circumstances we face.)

Gaining a Grasp on
JOHN'S GOSPEL

1. John's Gospel is possibly the *most evangelistic book* in the world. Its target is to bring people to living faith in Jesus. John was very specific in identifying his purpose in writing:

"But these are written that you may believe that Jesus is the Christ, the Son of God, and that believing you may have life in His name" John 20:31.

2. John's Gospel is the *chronological key* to the

Gospels, since the definite references he makes to three separate Passovers provide us with a grid of nearly 3 years to set forth Jesus' ministry. John 2:13, 23 note the first, which is shortly after the opening of His ministry; John 6:2 refers to a second, during His ministry; while John 12:1(et al) indicates the third and last Passover during His ministry, at which He was crucified. Many scholars feel that John 5:1 ("a feast of the Jews") may refer to a Passover also, which would bring the total season of Jesus' public ministry from somewhere in the late fall or early winter of 26/27 A.D., to Spring, 30 A.D.—about 3 1/2 years including the six weeks following His resurrection.

3. John's Gospel is *written by the Apostle John*, the brother of James. Both were Galilean fishermen before Jesus called them (Mark 1:19, 20). Throughout his Gospel, John never makes a direct reference to himself by name; but he chooses oblique phrases like "another disciple" (18:15); "that other disciple" (18:16; 20:3, 8); "that disciple whom Jesus loved" (21:20; 19:26). These references are brought to focus in 21:24, which designates the author as, "This is the disciple who testifies of these things…."

4. John's Gospel *sharply contrasts* with the common structure of the Synoptic Gospels (Matthew, Mark, and Luke). The first three basically provide a running commentary on the rise of Jesus' ministry, His focus on preaching, healing the sick, and casting out demons, and each also contains several of the parables Jesus used in His teaching ministry. John contains no parables and relates only to events involving approximately 20 distinct days in Jesus' entire

ministry (chapters 13-19—a full 1/3 of John—actually involve less than one 24-hour period).

5. John's Gospel *focuses three sets of sevens*, which provide the summary structural grid for his case intended to show the undeniability of Jesus' claim as the Messiah—Son of God. He presents *seven* "signs" (which are selected from the approximately 40 miracles specifically recorded of Jesus' ministry); *seven* "I Ams" (each of which declares a glorious facet of Jesus' person); and *seven* discourses (each one of which probes a distinct issue of faith which is either a question of the seeker or the problem of a critic).

6. John's Gospel opens with his *Prologue* (1:1-18), which many agree is one of the grandest literary pieces of all time. Like 1 Corinthians 13, Romans 8, Psalm 23, The Ten Commandments (Exodus 10:1-17), and The Beatitudes (Matthew 5:2-10), the Prologue to John deserves to be memorized by believers for its concise, yet brilliant, declaration of eternal truth.

7. John's Gospel more clearly features a primary *field of conflict* than it does a set of primary characters. While John the Baptist and Simon Peter each hold a prominent role at points in the book, the essential drama presents the evolving conflict and contrast between three groups and their response to Christ.

    (a) Jesus' disciples who followed Him
        (2:2; 3:22; 4:1; 6:3; 11:7; 13:22; et al);

    (b) "The Jews" who opposed Him
        (2:20; 5:16, 18; 7:1; 8:48; 9:18; 10:31; 11:54; 19:6, 7, 14, 15, et al); and

    (c) Various people, including many Jews, who

believed on Him (2:23; 4:42, 53; 7:31; 8:3l; 9:36; 10:42; 11:27; 12:11,42; et al).

8. John's Gospel is *sometimes criticized* for sounding anti-semitic because of the writer's frequent references to those leaders—usually generalized as "the Jews"—who opposed and then conspired to kill Jesus. But it must be remembered that (i) John was a Jew himself, and never turned against his people as a national entity. However, (ii) John's mood does reveal his frustration and disappointment with the leaders whose influence occasioned Jesus ultimately being rejected by so many of His own people. If this is misread as an ethnic attack, it is a misjudgment. Rather, John confronts the tragic fact that *so few* unfaithful leaders could *so unjustly* effect the confused response of *so many* they might have led to faith.

TWELVE KEY CONCEPTS—AN OVERVIEW OF
JOHN'S GOSPEL

The purpose of John's Gospel is to cause people to *believe*, to so clearly present the *Living Word* that people will follow Jesus Christ as the *Living Way*! The book is a testimony (21:24) intended to bring the reader to *know Jesus*—in person as the Savior of the world, as well as in factual knowledge as the Christ of Scripture. Twelve key concepts summarize the testimony of Jesus in John, and help direct us toward a full-dimensioned perspective on this Gospel and the Savior it depicts.

I. THE MISSION OF THE MASTER
Seeing the revealed purpose of Jesus' coming.

First, let us capture a sense of Jesus' purpose and pursuit in His ministry; recognizing He has called us not only to understand it, but to be at His service to be sent to extend and expand its the fulfillment of His mission (John 20:20).

1. To "Show" the Father

One of the most recurrent themes of John is established in verse 1:18 of the Prologue: "No one has seen God at any time. The only begotten Son…He has declared (Gk. *exegeomai*) Him." The meaning is profound, indicating a combination of purposes—*to explain, to describe, to tell, report or interpret.* So we are told that the first work of the Son was to so relate what Father God is like, that He might restore the broken image of His nature that has become fixed in fallen human minds.

Jesus makes frequent references to the fact that He says and does only "what the Father (says, does, gives Him, etc.)." Look up the following instances and notice how pointed the Savior is in His remarks as to His authentic role as "The Word" who expresses *only* the exact will of the Eternal Father God (5:19, 30; 6:38; 7:16; 8:28-29, 38a; 12:50b; 15:15, etc.).

In John 6:27, Jesus says, "the Father has set His seal on Him" (that is, on Jesus Himself). The word "seal" (Gk. *sphragidzo*) refers to the stamp of a signet ring, a private mark reserved under the control of a person to authenticate that any document so "sealed" is in fact fully authorized by and expressive of the will of the individual. So, in John, Jesus claims to be doing more than simply "speaking for" Father God, *He affirms that He is God—the Father's Son, and is the divinely sent, perfect expression of His Father's will and character!*

Read chapter 14:7-11, and note how absolutely Jesus declares His role as the Ultimate Representer/ Interpreter of the Father, as One in perfect communicative union with Him (10:30). In this light, apply the power of this truth to your own life. What, when, or where are instances or circumstances in which you are inclined to see God the Father as "different from" Jesus—in terms of His lovingness, His patience, His graciousness, His readiness to help, meet, forgive, heal, or strengthen you? Are you tempted to accept false imaginary ideas or feelings about God? For a practical exercise, make a list of 10 stories about Jesus (from any of the Gospels). Note in each a trait of divine love and grace Christ reveals; then, remember His words: *besides the action He is taking in those texts, He also wants to show you how the heart of the Heavenly Father feels toward us—toward YOU!*

2. To "Save" the World

"I did not come to judge the world but to save the world" (12:47) establishes the tone as well as the consummate target of Jesus' own description of His ministry. His *mission* of revealing the Father is aimed at achieving His *ministry* of rescuing lost human beings who will welcome His witness and work. "Jesus Saves" is still the heart of the Gospel we proclaim. To "save" (Gk. *sodzo*) is a deep and broad work of encompassing significance, incorporating multi-dimensional action: (a) *to deliver*, from bondage or oppression; (b) *to save*, from death or destruction; (c) *to cure*, from physical affliction or mental, emotional torment; (d) *to preserve or rescue, to bring out safely* from a hopeless situation. (Reread John 3:16-17 in the light of this full-orbed definition, as well as 5:34, 10:9—and review Matthew 18:11.)

3. To Bring Abundant Life

John 10:10 is one of the most quoted verses in the New Testament in which Jesus contrasts the will and goal of "<u>the</u> thief" (definite article indicates the reference is to the Devil), with the plan and purpose of "the good shepherd" (In verses 11 and 14 Jesus says <u>He</u> is describing Himself.) This passage defines "abundant" life (Gk. *perisseuo—more than enough, be left over.*) Jesus' discourse in John 10:1-14, shows *"life abundantly"* as that which—

a. Is accessed solely through "the Door" of His provision (verse 7)

b. Is experienced through following "the voice" of the Shepherd (verses 3, 4) and refusing to follow other ways (verse 5).

c. Is filled with plentiful protection ("saved") and provision ("find pasture") under the Shepherd's personal care (verse 9).

4. To "Judge" the Prince of this World

Jesus makes clear that He not only has come to rescue lost souls and bring His redeemed to fulfilled living as well as eternal life, He also announced His plan to break the power of the Devil: he will be "cast out" and "judged" (Gk. *krino, to be hauled before a court, condemned, and handed over for judicial punishment*). In other words, Jesus not only came to redeem humankind from the penalty of sin, He also came to release us from the power Satan gained over the world through the default of man when Adam fell.

The "fall" of man not only describes the break in his eternal relationship with God through his sin, but his lost "rule," or control, over the temporal matters of this world. In his first epistle (1 John 5:19) John says, "We know that we are of God, and the whole world lies under the sway of the wicked one" (Gk. *keimei, to be or find oneself in a certain state or condition*). The English word *"sway"* effectively conveys this idea, meaning "to rule, govern, exercise controlling influence, control or a preponderating force or pressure" (Webster). Jesus said the Holy Spirit's ministry would incorporate enforcing and applying this facet of His mission when accomplished (John 16:11). This truth is the foundation for the Church's authority over all dark powers, and for our proclaiming as Jesus did—"The Kingdom of God is at hand—here and now!" (See Ephesians 1:17-23; Matthew 24:14.)

II. THE MESSAGE OF THE MASTER
Communicating the revealed truth about Jesus

Jesus' *Mission* was achieved with such excellence because of the incalculable greatness of His own *being*. **He** is the *Message* He brought—*that's why He is called "THE WORD!"* For you and me to join

Christ in His mission, with His methods (to follow), we must be foremost clear and complete in our recognition of Who He *IS*—<u>the Incarnation of the Living God above all</u>! John sets forth:

5. The Ultimacy of Christ's Person

There is no more absolute statement of the ultimate issue at stake in recognizing the Person of Jesus Christ than His words, "If you do not believe that I am HE, you will die in your sins" (8:24). "HE" is Who He declares Himself to be; the fullness of which John sets forth in the great "I AM" statements of Jesus. (See the chart and references on page 14.)

6. The promise in Christ's Person

Each of the "I AM" titles of Christ is filled with meaning which Jesus intends to be understood. Because He is *the* "I AM," the Son of God (10:36), He is the Fulfiller of all God's promises (2 Cor. 1:20).

> …As the Bread of Life, *He is the Nourisher and Sustainer* of all God intends to be realized in each human being. He is the "Word" which has proceeded from the mouth of God, without which man cannot live (Matthew 4:4).
> …As the Light of the World, *He is the Revealer* of all we will ultimately know about God, and His presence brings the brilliance that extinguishes all controlling fear, error or blindness due to the Darkness.
> …As the Door of the Sheep, *He is the Access* to all promise and hope for life on earth or in heaven; affirming that any enterprises that

attempt other routes are illegal approaches
designed by the Thief (see John10:1;
Hebrews. 4:14-16).

…As the Good Shepherd, *He is the Protector
and Provider* for all who come to Him, and
thereby the One who assures "abundant" life.

…As the Resurrection and the Life, *He is the
Reviver and Restorer* who not only verifies the
future <u>hope of eternal life</u>, but declares His
present <u>power to restore loss</u>.

…As the Way, the Truth and the Life, *He is the
Discipler* of those who will to know His will;
unfolding the "how" (Way) to live, the "free-
dom" (Truth) to live, and the "fullness" (Life)
for living.

…As the True Vine, *He is the Fountainhead of
Fruitfulness* for those who come to Him;
opening the way to fellowship with Him
(15:4), to refinement through discipline
(15:2), and to effectiveness through obedience
(15:10, 16).

7. The Authority in Christ's Person

The seven discourses in John, in which Jesus
talks with groups or individuals and elaborates cen-
tral facts about Himself, are each worthy of exten-
sive study. Use this textual pointer to pursue your
own examination of the great truths Jesus discusses
about His authority in respect to each of these issues:

John 3:1-21 — He is God's Gift to mankind
and the watershed personality between light
and dark, truth and error.

John 4:3-26 — He is the only source of true satisfaction for humanity, and the final commentator on what constitutes true worship of the living God.

John 5:16-47 — He is the definer of the Law, the perfect expression of God's will and works, and the sole possessor of "life" and the right to ultimately pass judgment on any matters concerning mankind.

John 6:22-59 — He is the only source of eternal life, and He alone is granted the right of determination as to who shall be granted resurrection unto eternal life.

John 7:10-39 — He is the bringer of the New Covenant, which completes God's will as expressed in the Law, and opens to God's work within the human heart—releasing the life-flow of the Holy Spirit, according to the Old Testament prophecies (Ezekiel 11:19-20; 36:25-27; Isaiah 44:3-5).

John 8:13-59 — He is the Faithful and True Witness, who speaks with final authority because He precedes and exceeds all.

John 10:1-39 — He is the only true Shepherd of Israel, as well as of all mankind, and all other "voices" are of another source, for He alone is the SON OF GOD (verse 36). This final reference is the conclusive denial of any notion that Jesus ever perceived Himself as other than who He was—God's Son from Heaven, sent to earth to redeem mankind!

8. The Glory of Christ's Person

John begins and ends his Gospel with two such glorious declarations about the exceeding excellence of the person of Jesus Christ. No reader can miss the message: (a) Chapter 1:1-5—He is Creation's Mighty God, (b) Chapter 20, 21—He is Redemption's Risen Lord. The opening of the Prologue shows Jesus, the Word, as: (i) the pre-existent One, before all created things (verse 1a); (ii) equivalent with but distinct from the Father (verse 1b); (iii) present in eternal fellowship with the Father (verse 2); (iv) the conscious instrument of the creation of all things that exist (verse 4). In unmistakable terms, this passage declares, "Jesus of Nazareth is God!"

The climax of the Gospel is the Resurrection, and John cites unusual and convincing detail in relating individual cases of post-resurrection appearances of Jesus: (a) Mary Magdalene witnesses the phenomenon of the moved stone (20:1); (b) Peter and John visit the tomb and discover the witness of the grave clothes (20:2-10); (c) Mary sees the angels in the tomb, then encounters Jesus (20:11-18); (d) Ten disciples are visited by Jesus in the upper room (20:19-23); (e) Disciples, with Thomas present, are visited by Jesus (20:24-29); (f) Seven disciples are visited by Jesus at Galilee (21:1-23).

III. THE METHODS OF THE MASTER
Seeing the revealed patterns of Jesus' lifestyle

As with our gaining an understanding of Jesus'

Mission (for more than information or inspiration, but to be *sent* ourselves), and His *Message* (to assure clarity in describing the Person and the Gospel we preach), let us open to see, and to have developed for replication in our hearts, minds and living, the *ways*—the *Methods* by which Jesus ministers.

9. Manifests His Glory through "Signs"

John makes seven "miracles" or "signs" of Jesus' ministry the grid over which he develops his whole appeal to "believe" in Jesus (John 20:30-31). This is consistent with Jesus' own appeal to those who were angered by His claim to be the Son of God: "If I do not do the works of My Father, do not believe me; but if I do, though you do not believe Me, believe the works, that you may know and believe that the Father is in Me and I in Him."

The seven "signs" (Gk. *semeion—sign, distinguishing mark, wonder or miracle; a mark of genuineness*) John features are: Turning the water to wine (2:1-11); healing the nobleman's son (4:46-54); healing the man at the pool of Bethesda (5:1-15); feeding of the five thousand (6:1-14); walking on the sea (6:15-21); restoring sight to the man born blind (9:1-7); and the raising of Lazarus from the dead (11:1-47).

10. Relates to Individuals with Grace

Jesus "manner" as well as His "message" is so important. Though He is the Lord from Heaven, and endowed with all power and authority, there is a consistent gentleness and understanding toward the frailty of fallen man. He was not only full of *truth,* but full of *grace* as well (1:14): perhaps nothing is more commonly overlooked by the people of God. We are not only agents called to <u>transmit the facts</u> of a message, but we are representatives called to <u>show the love</u> that offers God's invitation to life. Take time to examine each of these episodes and note how Jesus...

- ...is affirming of the potential in people (1:42, 47)
- ...is gracious to help a wedding party avoid embarrassment (2:8)
- ...is tender in unveiling human failure (4:16-18)
- ...is faithful in following up (5:12-14)
- ...is concerned over basic human needs (6:5)
- ...is caring and assisting when struggles are faced (6:18-21)
- ...is forgiving of human sinning (8:7-12)
- ...is defending against ignorant accusations (9:3)
- ...is seeking toward the cast out (9:9-38)
- ...is compassionate at the presence of death (11:34-36)

(Study these textual settings and permit this quality of Jesus' ministry to help you see His manner in other situations in all the Gospels.)

11. Reveals Wisdom, Without Presumption

Even though Jesus is completely without cowardice, while also being wholly capable of any order of self-defending miracle, a remarkable trait is described by John. Jesus not only refuses to ever use a miracle to protect Himself, but He is frequently seen taking decisive steps to avoid collision with authorities or to unduly expose Himself to premature arrest or assault, or even preliminary exaltation by man. Note the following, and then search John's Gospel for additional cases of this sensitive, sensible feature of the Savior's style: 2:23-25; 4:1-3; 6:15; 7:1-10; 8:59; 10:39.

12. Lives with His Destiny Constantly in View

No fewer than 40 times in John's Gospel does Jesus refer to Himself as "sent" by the Father. His whole approach to His life is with a sense of commission—as one who has both a work (9:4a) to do and a season of time in which to fulfill it (9:4b). Another primary trait of John's record of Jesus' life, and which also clearly indicates Jesus' sense of His destiny, are references made to His "hour," that is, His appointed death on the Cross (2:4; 7:30; 8:20; 12:23, 27; 13:1; 16:21, 32; 17:1).

◆　　◆　　◆

All in all, the majesty of John's Gospel lies in the concise yet comprehensive way all these elements of Christ's life and His work are set forth—*stimulating* deep faith in the depths of His Person and the meaning of His ministry, and *summoning* to deep commitment to allow Him to fill and send us as His redeemed—into all the world, for which He died.

JESUS PRAYS

(1) For Himself: (vv. 1-5)	(2) For His disciples: (vv. 6-19)	(3) For future believers: (vv. 20-26)
He affirms the glory of the Cross (vv. 1, 2)	He prays for their knowledge (vv. 6-9)	He prays for their oneness (vv. 20-22)
He expresses the very essence of eternal life (vv. 3, 4)	He prays for their perseverance (vv. 10-12)	He prays for their perfect unity (v. 23)
He rejoices in the shared glory of the Father (v. 5)	He prays for their joy (v. 13)	He prays for their future presence with Him (vv. 24, 25)
	He prays for their sanctification (vv. 14-17)	He prays for their mutual love (v. 26)
	He prays for their mission (vv. 18, 19)	

PART 2

THE RELEVANT ANSWERS IN JOHN

SCOTT BAUER

ANSWERING QUESTIONS AND
SOLVING PROBLEMS

The Heart of the Savior
for People

This gospel opens a window for all to see a dimension of the Savior's personal care for people that is not as clearly present in the Synoptic Gospels (Matthew, Mark, Luke). You've heard the phrase, "If it's too good to be true, it is." That may apply to people, but not to God. John shows us a compassionate Savior who is supremely patient with people who struggle, instantly available to the needy, and always willing to outflank the prevailing wisdom of the religious culture in order to reflect the nature and heart of the Father.

John provides portraits of Jesus in real conversation with individuals, which completely obliterate the notion of an ecclesiastical hierarchy concerned about its own self-preservation. The consistent picture the Gospel presents is Jesus' unqualified concern for the individual and His willingness to meet him or her at the crisis point of need. In this context, Jesus removes religious error with surgical precision and confronts sin with boldness. He identifies the intents of the heart with a discernment which confounds the human proclivity toward mixing motives and attempting to seize a moral advantage in situations. Jesus loves people and He mirrors the heart of the Father to all.

There are at least nine substantial conversations recorded with people who each encounter Jesus at crisis moments. These offer tremendous insight into both the human condition and the heavenly resource needed to break through to God's purpose with each person.

Nathaniel, 1:45-51:
Knowing The Seeking Heart

Jesus' supernatural understanding of Nathaniel's experience under the fig tree was evidence enough of Jesus' place as "Son of God!" and "King of Israel!" verse 49. Whatever the issue of concern, only God could possibly have known the cry of Nathaniel's heart. Jesus' response characterizes God's concern for and knowledge of every person.

Nicodemus, 3:1-21:
Removing Religious Blindness

The fact that Nicodemus came to Jesus at night typifies the religious bondage which disallows honest inquiry among the "faithful." The Pharisees would have rejected Nicodemus' action as traitorous following the cleansing of the Temple—2:13-22. His conversation with Jesus focuses on the new birth by faith. Old religious notions of justification through religious ceremony clash with the dynamic truth of a transformation from within by the Holy Spirit. "For God so loved the world that He gave

His only begotten Son, that whoever believes in Him should not perish but have everlasting life. For God did not send His Son into the world to condemn the world, but that the world through Him might be saved." The universal availability of God's grace (whoever), the power of personal faith in God (believes), and the insistence on God's unwillingness to condemn (he who does not believe is condemned) all witness to a radical departure from conventional religious dogma. Jesus opens Nicodemus' eyes to a world of faith and hope.

Samaritan Woman, 4:4-26:
Confronting Bigotry and Human Brokenness

The encounter is summed up by the phrase "He (Jesus) needed to go through Samaria." His only mission in Samaria was to talk with one woman who was morally bankrupt and ethnically hostile. In His extended conversation with her, Jesus bridges the weakness of human sin and the racial separatism that divides people from the true heart of God. God loves sinners, and welcomes them to new life in Him, and Jesus breaks ethnic and racial stereotyping by appealing to the true nature of man's need for and desire of God (verses 13-14). Jesus' instruction to the woman confounds both the Samaritan and Jewish religious establishments and redefines the essence of a relationship with the living God (verses 21-26).

Paralytic at Bethsaida, 5:2-15:
Relieving Suffering

The paralytic lay helplessly at the pool of

Bethsaida. Jesus' question seems odd and insensitive—"Do you want to be made well?" After 38 years of suffering, the answer should be obvious. However, the human capacity for self-pity and the accommodating of bondage render this an incisive and critical question. God's ability to touch circumstance where health is not welcomed is limited. This passage also illustrates Jesus' unwillingness to be restricted by the legalistic maintenance of religious habit (humanly devised rules for the Sabbath) at the expense of human need.

Adulteress and Her Accusers, 8:1-12: Exposing Hypocrisy

The woman was taken "in the very act." Curiously, she just happens to be discovered while her male partner seems to have vanished. This is a set-up devised by scribes and Pharisees who may have procured her services or, at least, were well acquainted with them. Their complete willingness to expose her shame and condemn her to death is contrasted by the Lord's refusal to condemn her and His defense of her against detractors. Jesus' scrawlings in the dirt (verse 6) seem to have convicted the self-righteous and silenced their calls for "justice." Jesus is, once again, the friend of sinners and His entreaty to "go and sin no more" is not a license for the flesh, but a sobering start for a hope-filled second chance.

Blind Man, 9:1-41: Challenging Self-Righteousness

The disciples questioned Jesus concerning the

blind man—"Who sinned?" (verse 2). The rigid, loveless application of a spiritual principle can infect Pharisee and Disciple alike. Jesus recasts the question by asserting that God is to be revealed in the matter, and that the true interest of the inquiry should be directed toward the man's healing. The anger of the Pharisees at the healing is more than a matter of Sabbath offense, it is a rejection of God's work at meeting human need. Even today, wherever Jesus heals there are those who reject God's work and indict those who pray for and minister the healing touch of God.

Mary and Martha, 11:17-57:
Overcoming Death

Martha (verse 21), Mary (verse 32), and the gathering crowd (verse 37) all blame Jesus for Lazarus' death. The compassionate Savior neither accepts their words as true nor attacks them for faithlessness. "I am the resurrection and the life" was His response to Martha—the message: believe in Me! Jesus wept over the hopelessness of people in the face of death and their inability to understand His love and power at the most crucial moment in their lives. Jesus resurrects Lazarus and demonstrates His dominion over death, and once again the religious establishment has no stomach for His compassionate and miraculous work. In fact, this resurrection crystallizes the resolve of Jesus' enemies to destroy Him.

Thomas, 20:24-29:
Dissolving Doubt

Peter and John were convinced of Jesus' resurrection at the empty tomb. Thomas, upon hearing their report, was not. Eight days after Thomas' dramatic declaration of needing to see and touch the Lord's nail prints, he touched them in behalf of all those for all time who must see and touch to believe. Doubt ingrains itself in the human circumstance as our experience cautions us against hope. Jesus' words in verse 29 assert the righteousness of faith which discerns between false trust in man and belief in the living God.

Peter, 21:5-24:
Obeying God's Call

The disciple who three times denied Him is now three times charged with the care of the flock. Upon receiving this mission and understanding the terms of its pursuit (Peter's death, verse 19), Peter inquires about John's mission and future. "What is that to you? Follow Me." Jesus' pointed retort defines our personal ministry, its methodology, and its results as being His responsibility to direct. "Follow Me" is the universal call for every disciple. Ministries are not to be compared or placed in competition with each other—it is Christ's Church and Kingdom. He will direct us as it pleases Him.

Conclusion

Jesus' awareness of human weakness, resistance, and fear translates directly into compassion, confrontation, and comfort in His dealings with individuals. Jesus never sacrifices truth by indulging human failure, but He never fails to fully consider the human emotions, limitations, and experiences which predispose people toward doubt or faith. There are no formulae by which Jesus mechanically relates to souls who seek Him. The truth of God's Word circumscribes the boundaries of our relationship to God, but it is the Holy Spirit who applies the healing touch of Jesus to the unique circumstances in our personal world. It is this consummate concern for the individual which characterizes the whole of Jesus' ministry. In the Gospel of John, Jesus has time for people; He has concern for their troubles; He has answers which secure eternal destiny in the midst of current trial.

Jesus is as knowledgeable and considerate of us as we could ever dream—and more. If He seems to be too good to be true, it is because "the Word became flesh and dwelt among us." God has come to us. Love sent Him so that we might know Him.

QUESTIONS IN
JOHN'S GOSPEL

There are five recurring questions in this gospel which deserve particular attention. Two of the questions are textual and relate directly to the authenticity of the Gospel. The other three open the way for theological speculation which has proliferated exaggerated doctrines of ecclesiastical dominance within sectors of the Church and fueled error in cult groups outside of the Body of Christ.

Resolving these questions offers both a framework for analyzing Scriptural challenges by those who contest its veracity, and it addresses the perversion of Truth for the purpose of advancing false and unbiblical patterns of worship. The undermining of the authority of Scripture is the fastest way to deplete vital faith in Christ. Demonic assault on the Bible has continued in every generation, yet the text of Scripture has proven true and trustworthy in every test. However, an even greater evil is the exaggeration of Scripture and sanctioning of additional extraneous materials as equal in authority to the Bible. Every cult group seizes on the authority of the Bible and then seeks to reinterpret and add to Scripture "further revelation." In addressing the questions in John, these extraneous materials are directly discredited as false and destructive.

Cleansing the Temple, 2:13-22

John records the cleansing of the Temple at the beginning of Jesus' ministry. This contrasts with the account in the Synoptic Gospels. The question: Were there two Temple cleansings or is John mistaken about the timing? Only John is an eyewitness to this portion of Jesus' ministry. Luke did not have firsthand knowledge of Jesus; Mark is presumed to be found at the end of his gospel account in Mark 14:51-52; Matthew was the last of Jesus' disciples to be called and joined Him in Capernaum in Matthew 9:9. Only John would have been present to witness this cleansing of the Temple. Clearly, there were two separate occurrences. John did not have a memory failure, and Matthew was present at the Temple cleansing at the *end* of Jesus' ministry. In fact, John's record explains the almost immediate hostility of religious authorities toward Jesus and His ministry. The miracles and healings were a testimony to the righteousness of Jesus' actions in the Temple in John 2.

The Adulteress, 7:53-8:11

This account in the ministry of Jesus has been challenged in its authenticity because of its absence in certain of the most ancient manuscripts used for Bible translation. In fact, some translations of Scripture only include this passage in a footnote to the text. Others bracket the material with notation. Some commentators refuse to include it in their work on the Gospel of John. The text is challenged because, in addition to its absence in a few manuscripts, there are certain unique phrases found in the passage which are presumed to verify the rightness of challenging its place in the Gospel record as an unwarranted addition by later editors. And, in the writings of the early Church Fathers, there is doubt as to its veracity.

However, there are over 900 ancient manuscripts which *do* include this text. Augustine writes that some early manuscripts expunged this passage from the text because of the fear of promoting sexual impurity. The "Textus Receptus," upon which The King James Version was translated, includes this passage. This manuscript is affirmed by many scholars as the preferred and authentic text by which all others should be compared.

In fact, the rejection of this passage is an object lesson in the life of the Church that in the face of an overwhelming number of texts which affirm its truth, the text is still rejected. The account of the woman taken in adultery is a challenge to our understanding of the holiness of God. Such grace is difficult to accept by some. However, the account is totally within the character of our Lord, and is consistent with His confounding the false spirituality of those who protect the Lord and His Church from sin by limiting His grace. Human energy and withholding of grace can never keep the Church holy. It is the work of the Holy Spirit transforming the lives of people that makes true holiness an advancing reality in the life of the Church.

"Other Sheep," 10:16

This rather vague reference of Jesus has been used to create a variety of theories about everything from lost peoples to extraterrestrials. Several groups outside the Body of Christ claim special revelation for the interpretation of the text which has absolutely no relationship to the text itself or even the stated intent of the passage concerning Jesus—the Good Shepherd.

The verse refers to Jesus as the Lord of the Gentiles as well as the Lord of the Jews. He is the Good Shepherd to all people who respond to Him by faith. In the racially divided environment of the first century, it was inconceivable to many Jews that the Gentiles would have any place in the heart or plan of God. Here, Jesus corrects this mistaken notion.

Ecclesiastical Authority, 20:23

"If you forgive the sins of any, they are forgiven

them; if you retain the sins of any, they are retained." These dramatic words are the first spoken to the disciples following Jesus' bestowal of the Spirit on them. This commission was given not only to those present, but to all who believe in Christ. It is the function of the Body of Christ to convey the message of salvation and to confirm the forgiveness of sin to those who believe.

Historically, the Church hierarchy has abused this power by administrating forgiveness on the basis of traditions and policies which were uninformed by the Bible. In fact, withholding Communion for violation of Church polity is a traditional means of disciplining wayward members. However, this was often more a political or financial matter than a spiritual one.

This awesome power was never to be the singular province of priests, bishops, or popes. The Bible declares that we are all a "royal priesthood, a holy nation" (1 Peter 2:9), and as such, we are privileged to minister forgiveness to those who truly repent and believe.

"Other Gospels," 20:30; 21:25

John affirms that the acts of Jesus are not completely contained in the fourth gospel or, for that matter, in the first three. In fact, "I suppose that even the world itself could not contain the books that would be written" (21:25). John wrote this concerning everything Jesus said and did. This opens the door to wholly illegitimate speculation by those who have "another gospel." Paul in Galatians 1:9 pronounces anathema on those who present "any other gospel." This is true in terms of both a perversion of what is already revealed in Scripture, and in the introduction of spurious texts which have not been validated by the work of the Holy Spirit in the Church and their retention in the canon of Scripture.

The fact that there is more to Jesus' life and ministry than what has been revealed in Scripture is no surprise to anyone. However, the purpose of the biblical revelation of the life of Christ is exceedingly clear in John 20:31—"These are written that you may believe that Jesus is the Christ, the Son of God, and that believing you may have life in His name." The canon of Scripture and, specifically, this Gospel of John provide all that is necessary for a person to experience the saving grace of God by faith. That was Jesus' purpose in coming to earth—"But as many as received Him, to them He gave the right to become children of God, even to those who believe in His name" (John 1:12).

The claim of false religions to other sacred writings always violates the biblical revelation of Jesus as God's only Son and "the way, the truth, and the life" (John 14:6). False religions reject the exclusive claims of Jesus Christ as the only Mediator of salvation. And they proclaim a human-based belief structure which ultimately rejects Christ and leads to destruction.

Conclusion

The integrity and exclusive nature of the Bible is essential to our life in Christ. The Word of God is not just a standard for our lifestyle, it is the final authority for all we believe and it is the absolute arbiter in what we experience of His grace. Our experience with Jesus Christ, the Word *(Logos)* of God, is made real to us by the Holy Spirit, and is solely related to the things revealed in Scripture. Our experience must be consistent with the truth of God's Word, the Bible. Anything in contradiction to that Word is invalid. Anything outside the scope of the Bible is speculation which eventually leads to spiritual confusion and death.

Therefore, our stance toward the Bible is filled with faith and certainty—the Bible is true and trustworthy. We believe what it says, and live according to its directive.

THE WORK OF THE HOLY SPIRIT IN
JOHN'S GOSPEL

John presents the Holy Spirit with precision not attested to in the other gospels. He separates the work of the Holy Spirit in a person's life into two distinct categories. The first has to do with the work of the Holy Spirit in new birth and salvation (3:1-21; 14:17; 20:22). The second has to do with the Holy Spirit's power at work through God's people for witness and ministry (1:33; 15:26-27; 16:8-14). The first category of Holy Spirit activity is described by the phrase "You must be born again" (3:7). The second category of the Holy Spirit's activity is clearly declared in 1:33—"this is He (Jesus) who baptizes with the Holy Spirit."

The Holy Spirit
and New Birth

"That which is born of the flesh is flesh, that which is born of Spirit is spirit" (3:6). We have all experienced the physical birth of flesh. However, every person needs to be "born again" (3:3). John clearly identifies these people in 1:13—"who were born, not of blood, nor of the will of the flesh, nor of the will of man, but of God." This is accomplished by the work of the Holy Spirit. However, the availability of a person to such new birth is directly related to faith in Jesus Christ (3:16-18).

The new birth is supernaturally administered by the Holy Spirit as we place our faith in Jesus Christ. Our salvation is accomplished through what Jesus has done for us on the Cross, and it is administered to us by the Holy Spirit who dwells in us by faith (14:17). It is the dynamic integration of two transcendent truths which declare the magnificence of our being born again. First, our new birth is not a matter of our will—it is a matter of God's will (1:13). At the same time, it requires our confirmation of God's will to appropriate His purpose in our lives through faith (3:16). Our eternal salvation is secured in the will of God and activated by our believing in Christ.

Holy Spirit Baptism

"This is He who baptizes with the Holy Spirit" (1:33). John the Baptist's declaration occurs at the time of Jesus' water baptism. We know from the other Gospels that, at the time of Jesus' baptism in water, the Holy Spirit was bestowed on Him. This empowering was necessary for Him to conduct His ministry to the world. And, in this verse, this same empowering work of the Holy Spirit is also promised to us.

This work of the Spirit is referenced in 7:38-39 as something that would occur in the life of the believer after Jesus' glorification. It occurred after Christ's Ascension on the Day of Pentecost when the infant Church was "baptized with the Spirit" (Acts 1:5). In John 7:38-39, the promise of this work of the Holy Spirit is that it will not only happen *within you* but it will also flow *out of you* to others.

Jesus reinforces this second outflowing work of the Holy Spirit in a person's life by describing the activity of testifying of Christ (15:26-27). This is done directly *by* the Holy Spirit, and *through* the lives of those who have been Spirit-empowered to bear witness of Christ. The evidence of Pentecost amply demonstrates how this was accomplished in the life of the Church.

John 16:5-15 is a window into the working of the Holy Spirit through His empowered people. "I will send Him to you" (16:7). This is the promise of 1:33 reiterated through the lips of the Savior. And the mission of the Holy Spirit is very clear: "Convict the world" (16:8). That is why the Holy Spirit is being sent to the people of God: because "they (the unbelieving world) do not believe in Me" (16:9). Obviously, those who have received the Holy Spirit have believed. However, it is for the sake of those who do not believe that the Holy Spirit baptism occurs. The Church is to be empowered for supernatural witness in the Holy Spirit.

Yet, there is another dimension to this Spirit Baptism which will occur. "When He, the Spirit of truth, has come, He will guide you into all truth" (16:13). There is an interactive and highly personal dimension of the work of the Holy Spirit in a person's life. Repeatedly, Jesus uses the phrase "the Helper" for the Holy Spirit. This interaction with the Holy Spirit is to benefit the believer in every area of life and ministry. From rivers of living water flowing out of the heart (7:38) to "God is Spirit, and those who worship Him must worship in spirit and truth" (4:24), this personal dimension of the relationship with the Holy Spirit requires an openness to the Lord and a trust in what He will do in us by the Holy Spirit.

For many in the Church, the work of the Holy Spirit is limited to the most vital task of salvation and the advancing character development of those who have surrendered to Christ. And there is more! Jesus intends His Church to be a dynamic force in the world. Filled with His Spirit, the Body of Christ will testify to God's goodness and minister the salvation of God to the whole world with unlimited Holy Spirit power.

PART 3

PRACTICAL WISDOM FROM JOHN

JACK HAMILTON

THE DEATH OF JESUS

	Aspect of Jesus' Death	Old Testament Reference
The Jews viewed Jesus' death as a scandal.	In obedience to His Father (18:11)	Psalm 40:8
	Announced by Himself (18:32; see 3:14)	Numbers 21:8,9
The church understood His death as fulfillment of Old Testament prophecy.	In the place of His people (18:14)	Isaiah 53:4-6
	With evildoers (19:18)	Isaiah 53:12
	In innocence (19:6)	Isaiah 53:9
	Crucified (19:18)	Psalm 22:16
	Buried in a rich man's tomb (19:38-42)	Isaiah 53:9

ENCOUNTERS WITH LIVING
LOVE

LOOKING INTO JOHN

John had a fixation. He had a particular view of Jesus that exposed the heart of God. In the course of his writings he could have chosen to expound on any of the changeless attributes of the Father. Instead, John is very focused. When reading the things that this beloved apostle wrote, a person quickly encounters the theme of God's love.

After a lifetime of committed service to Jesus Christ, it is clear that it was God's love, revealed in the Savior, that most impacted John.

Love for John.

Love for His people.

Love for the world He created.

And most assuredly, love for sinners He came to rescue and save.

In his first epistle, John makes a declaration that explodes with revelation. Love is of God. **God is love** (1 John 4:7-8). This truth is at the heart of what he corresponds to people concerning Jesus. The love of God is clearly manifest in Christ and his account of what Jesus did and said is ripe with this proposition. Every encounter with the Son of God that he writes about has as its underpinnings in the loving touch of God that reaches from heaven by the hand of Jesus.

There is so much material to record concerning all that Jesus did demonstrating the Father's love that the whole world could not contain all the books that could be written (John 21:25). He writes because he was captured by a loving Savior, and for over six decades John had been a beneficiary of God's love through Christ. He witnessed many times the magnificent signs of Christ's redemptive power, each one energized by the love of God bringing everlasting life to those who believed in Him. Therefore, the stated purpose of John's record is… "That you may believe that Jesus is the Christ, the Son of God, and that believing you should have life in His name" (John 20:31).

The availability of such an awesome and wonderful reality is found in the words of Jesus: "For God so loved the world that He gave His only begotten Son, that whoever believes in Him should not perish but have everlasting life" (John 3:16). By recording this statement in the middle of the dialog between Jesus and Nicodemus, John forever settles the question of what motivates God and Christ to pursue and redeem fallen humanity. People will be impacted by many events, emotions, and experiences in their lifetimes. Nothing, however, will have as lasting an affect on them as will the encounter with Jesus, who is the love of God personified. That is what John does by the inspiration of the Holy Spirit. He tells everyone that this Divine Love is now encased in human form. Love can now be observed, heard, and touched. And when He is encountered, no one remains the same. Love never fails (1 Corinthians 13:8).

God will not fail when there are no resources left (John 2:3). He will not fail when there is confusion and wonder (John 3:2-5). He will not fail the thirsty soul (John 4:7-14). He will not fail the crippled (John 5:8). He will not fail the hungry or the frightened (John 6:8-11,19-20). He will not fail the honest inquirer (John 7:16-17). He will not fail the exposed sinner (John 8:10-11). He will not fail the blinded (John 9:6-7, 25, 35-38). He will not fail as the Shepherd of souls (John 10:27-28). He will not fail the bereaved (John 11:25-26, 43-44). He will not fail those in the dark (John 12:44-46). He will not fail to demonstrate the spirit of true service (John 13:13-15). He will not fail the troubled (John 14:1-6, 27). He will not fail to offer true friendship (John 15:12-17). He will not fail to give a Helper (John 16:7-14). He will not fail to intercede (John 17). He will not fail His own test (John 18:38). He will not fail in dying (John 19:30, 35). He will not fail to assure disbelief (John 20:24-29). And finally, He will not fail to restore (John 21:15-19).

At one time or another, everyone has had the need for the intervention of Jesus in their behalf. It matters not whether Christ has been embraced. Human beings are so vulnerable that they are easily overcome by the issues of living out their lives. For the most part, things are very normal. And then suddenly life becomes complex and confusing. John points out that the believer in Christ or the unbeliever will have many of the same emotions and experiences. The apostle reports how the Lord met people in need. These episodes encourage everyone to embrace Jesus in order to process life's ups and downs. John inscribes these words of Jesus to emphasize His loving care. "These things I have spoken to you, that in Me you may have peace. In the world you will have tribulation; but be of good cheer, I have overcome the world" (John 16:33).

LOVE'S INCARNATION

No mystery of life is more intriguing than that of God encased in humanity. The idea seems so incomprehensible. Yet that is exactly what happened. "Veiled in flesh the Godhead see, hail the incarnate Deity. Pleased as man with men to dwell, Jesus our Emmanuel…" The lyrics from this Christmas carol say it very well. *Emmanuel!* God with us. The Creator becoming the creature, while maintaining all He is. Who can really fathom this miracle? But then, miracles are not truly explainable. They can only be experienced.

When God as Jesus comes on the scene, it is the ultimate miracle expression of His love for people. Love will be demonstrated in many ways as Jesus empathizes with the needs of people and does something about them: healing, delivering, providing, comforting. Christ will even die for the sins of humanity. He will rise from the dead to secure their hope forever. All of these acts happened because of God's love for people. And they would not have happened if God did not come to live among us in human flesh. Love became incarnate in the God-man Jesus of Nazareth.

1. Identifying the Word (John 1:1,14,17).
   a. The Word was God (verse 1).
   b. The Word became flesh, full of grace and truth (verse 14).
   c. Grace and truth came by Jesus Christ (verse 17).
   d. The Word and Jesus Christ are the same person.

2. Identified in the World (John 1:19-34).
   a. Jesus identified as the preferred One (verses 21-27, 30).
   b. Jesus identified as the "Lamb of God" (verse 29).
   c. Jesus identified as the One Who baptizes with the Holy Spirit (verses 32-33).

LOVE'S PROVISION

Have you ever felt empty? Have you ever been broke—with no income? Have you ever been really hungry with no prospect of a meal? Each of these conditions is a common human experience. There are times when emotions are spent and there isn't anything left with which to feel. The tank of the soul is depleted. An overwhelming sense of numbness dominates the mind. In times like these, a person just wants to run some place and hide, but there is not anywhere to go because the emptiness is not a matter of geography. The feeling is internal, not external. Sometimes despair is so great that death seems the only alternative. The emotions are real and raw. The solution is foolish.

And what about the times that the bills exceeded the bank account? The pressure of threatening letters from creditors creates both anger and fear. The telephone calls from the collection agency force a compromise to telling the truth—"The check is in the mail." This condition can result from the loss of a job, overusing easy credit available, or not being disciplined in budget management. The lack of resources can be very stressful; however, it is not the end of the world.

No matter what people face, there is One who will supply all their needs (Philippians 4:19). John chronicles many occasions when Jesus was able to provide for people in need. The Lord not only met people's needs in ancient days, but He continues to offer resources for men and women in contemporary times. Caring for people is what God does best, and whenever Jesus acts, He expresses the will of a loving Father (John 6:38).

1. Provision When Nothing Is Left (John 2:1-10).
   a. Resources people have are limited (verse 3).
   b. Resource repletion requires obedience to God's Word (verse 5).
   c. Resource provided by God requires change (verses 7-9).
   d. Resource from God is always the best (verse 10).

2. Provision When Things Appear Overwhelming (John 6:1-13).
   a. The Lord is aware of human needs (6:5).

    b.   The Lord uses what people offer Him (6:9-11).

    c.   The Lord provides abundantly (6:12-13). Cf. John 10:10.

3.   Provision When Fear Is Dominating (6:15-21).

    a.   Fear is bred in darkness and Jesus is not apparently present (6:17).

    b.   Fear dominates when things get out of control (6:18-19b).

    c.   Fear is replaced when Jesus is willingly received (6:19a-21).

4.   Provision When Hope Is Lost (John 11:1-44).

    a.   Hope seems compromised by death (11:14, 21, 32).

    b.   Hope is strengthened through faith in Christ (11:25-27, 40).

    c.   Hope is restored through prayer (11:41-42).

    d.   Hope is realized at the command of Jesus (11:43-44).

LOVE'S INTERACTION

In his first epistle John writes, "Let us not love in word or in tongue, but in deed and truth" (1 John 3:18). He is not stating a simple admonition based only in reason. This declaration is substantial because he witnessed how true love is expressed. Love is not a statement of affection, but it is a demonstration of caring interaction with the person loved. Time after time while in the presence of Jesus he witnessed the acts of compassion done by the Savior. Christ was not inconvenienced when He saw the dilemma of the human soul. In the love of God He reached out to hurting humanity. Christ not only said He loved people, He constantly and consistently demonstrated love for them.

While John gives a record of the acts of the love of Jesus, the testimony of the expressions of His love continues in the present time. It is truly amazing that in the most compelling of circumstances an individual may encounter the Lord and experience the love of God. Sometimes it is the direct action of God. Most of the time, however, it is the indirect acts of His love through someone who has been captured by that Love and in His name expresses the continuing flow of God's care and concern. Just as Jesus' coming allowed people to engage the love of God in a tangible fashion, so those encased in Christ are able to continue the tangibility of God's love. These actions are not optional. They are mandated by the new commandment given by Jesus, "A new commandment I give to you, that you love one another; as I have loved you, that you also love one another" (John 13:34).

If mankind is to know God loves them, they must encounter that love. Jesus led the way and He said for us to follow Him. When we do, the result will be a multiplication of people who realize that God does love them, and in this the Father will be glorified (John 14:12-13).

1. Love Interacts With Physical Limitations (John 5:1-9; 9:1-38).

a. Love helps when no one else will (5:7).
b. Love helps when the way and time are unconventional (5:8-9).
c. Love is concerned with the condition, not the reason (9:2-3).
d. Love's acts release faith and worship (9:35-38).

2. Love Interacts With the Soul's Dilemma (John 8:1-11; 13:37-38; 18:17, 25-27; 21:15-19).
   a. Love understands human frailty and guilt (8:4, 7; 13:37-38).
   b. Love does not condemn (8:10-11; 18:17, 25-27; 21:15-18).
   c. Love affirms and asks for the best (8:11; 21:19).

3. Love Interacts With Spiritual Pursuit (John 3:1-21; 4:1-30, 39-42).
   a. Love is patient with inquiry (3:4; 4:11, 20).
   b. Love offers new life and salvation (3:13-17; 4:22-26).
   c. Love reveals the Savior (3:17; 4:42).

LOVE'S INTERCESSION

Many times there is need for another to intervene on someone's behalf: the friend who will make the introduction to an attractive other; the letter written to recommend an applicant for a new position or job; the attorney who pleads a client's cause; the accountant who represents another in a tax audit.

Personal limitations are a reality in today's complex world. Having someone available to assist from time to time is a true consolation. Knowing that problems are not faced alone prevents stress and anxiety from ruling the day.

John overheard a prayer. Its content gave him strength for his lifetime of service to the Lord and His Church. Imagine the times when the apostle's faith was tested. He was weary from hardship. He lamented over rejection and persecution. He did not like the role of arbitrating division among brothers. It's not difficult to picture him relying on the words of intercession he heard coming from that olive grove so long ago. Jesus was earnestly praying for all who call upon Him as Savior. John's remembrance of that prayer put steel in his backbone and resolve in his soul. And his report is that this prayer is for others too. The writer of the Book of Hebrews says it this way, "He is also able to save to the uttermost…since He ever lives to make intercession…" (Hebrews 7:25). Jesus, the manifestation of God's love, interceded in the Garden, interceded on the Cross, and is interceding in Heaven right now! Oh yes, and this exercise is for all people for all time.

1. The Object of Intercession (John 17:1-5).
   a. The authority to give eternal life (verses 2-3).
   b. The glorifying of the Father and His Son Jesus (verses 4-5).

2. The Subject of Intercession (John 17:6-26).
    a. The presentation of the saved by Jesus (verses 6-10).
    b. The preservation of the saved from the world (verses 11-19).
    c. The purity of the saved (verses 20-26).

LOVE'S SACRIFICE

John was at Calvary. He witnessed first-hand the battered and beaten body of Jesus, the Lord fastened to the Cross by spikes in His hands and feet. His Master was suspended between Heaven and earth on that cruel tree. With his arm around the Savior's mother, he was commissioned to care for her. At the moment it must have been the darkest day he ever experienced. Later he would write, "Greater love has no one than this, than to lay down one's life for his friends" (John 15:13). He would stay until the end. He heard the cry, "It is finished!" (John 19:30), not completely understanding that the price for the sins of all people had been completely paid.

It was not the nails that kept Jesus on the Cross. It was not the Roman soldiers performing their ugly duty (John 19:11). It was Love. The Baptist had proclaimed this event approximately 36 months before. John heard the camel hair-clothed prophet say, "Behold! The Lamb of God who takes away the sin of the world!" (John 1:29). And this was exactly what was taking place on Golgotha. Love's sacrifice was making it possible for people to live without sin's deadly affect. Guilt is eradicated with the cry of forgiveness from the Cross. No more sacrifice is needed. This full measure of love and devotion is complete salvation then and now!

1. Love's Sacrifice Fulfills Recorded Prophecy (John 19:17-37).
   a. Crucified among thieves and pierced (19:17-24). Cf. Psalm 22:16-18.
   b. Crucified to accomplish the Scriptures (19:28-37). Cf. Psalm 22:15; 34:20; Zechariah 12:10.

2. Love's Sacrifice Accomplishes the Divine Plan (John 19:30). Cf. John 1:29; Revelation 13:8.

LOVE'S TRIUMPH

The most profound report made in the Gospel of John is the incarnation. God became man. Jesus Christ is that man. Throughout this gospel, signs are recorded verifying His identity—miracles of healing, overcoming natural laws, and raising Lazarus from the dead. All were signs that a Man with Divine qualities and characteristics was among humanity. Why He had come remained a mystery to most. The life He led caused a controversy for many. In an attempt to eliminate His influence He was crucified. His disciples were devastated. His enemies elated. None could have comprehended that when He declared, "I am the resurrection and the life" (John 11:25), He was preparing people for the ultimate sign as to Who was living with them.

The crucifixion was not the end of Jesus—it was the beginning for all people. His death and burial formed the seedbed of salvation. And the fruit of salvation exploded out of the tomb with the same force with which the universe had been created.

The resurrection of Jesus from the dead is a proclamation of His purpose. The final enemy of all has been overcome. Eternal life is available for anyone who will roll away the stone of their heart to let Jesus the Savior in. It is not just an empty tomb that validates the resurrection of Christ. It is also the appearance of the resurrected Lord Jesus to the faithful who had followed and believed in Him. In His reassurances to them, He offers His blessing to all generations—like the people who read this booklet.

1. The Evidence of Love's Triumph (John 20:1-10).
   a. An empty tomb (verses 1-2).
   b. Empty burial garments (verses 3-8).

2. The Witnesses of Love's Triumph (John 20:11-18).
   a. The testimony of angels (verses 11-13).
   b. The testimony of Mary (verses 14-16,18).
   c. The testimony of Jesus (verse 17).

3. The Result of Love's Triumph (John 20:19-29).
   a. A blessed peace (verse 19).
   b. A blessed mission (verse 21).
   c. A blessed gift (verse 22).
   d. A blessed challenge (verse 23).
   e. A blessed confession (verses 28-29).

A FINAL THOUGHT ON LOVE

Throughout John's gospel he refers to himself as the *other disciple* or *another disciple*; however, insight into how he felt about his relationship with Jesus is found in chapter 13, verse 23. He writes," *…one of His disciples, whom Jesus loved.*" John was that disciple. Did Jesus love John more than the others? No. The fact, however, that John could sense the Savior's love for him must have been very reassuring. As a consequence, God's love became a principal subject for him and it permeates all that he records.

It seems clear that everyone is loved by God, and that He proclaimed that blessed reality by sending Jesus. Jesus manifested God's love by reaching out to people and going to the Cross in their place. Christ also encouraged all who believed in Him to love others as He loved them. Too difficult? Well, it will demand relinquishing some prejudices and biases. It may mean setting aside some personal agenda items. It *will* require the death of selfishness in order for love to rise in prominence.

How is Love known?

By giving oneself to Jesus.

How is love developed?

By following the example of Jesus.

A contemporary proverb is based on the story John tells in Chapter 6 about the hungry multitude. ***"Love is like five loaves and two fishes. It is never enough until it is given away."*** Jesus loves and He makes all who will receive Him a lover of God…and of people too.

A unique travel video
that makes the Gospels spring to life!

WALK WHERE JESUS WALKED

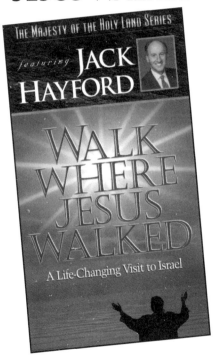

With Jack Hayford as your guide, you'll see the same sights that Jesus showed to His followers. A beautiful and inspiring one-hour plus presentation.

WWJWV $24.99

A practical study in the gospel of John!

SPRINGTIME STUDIES IN JOHN

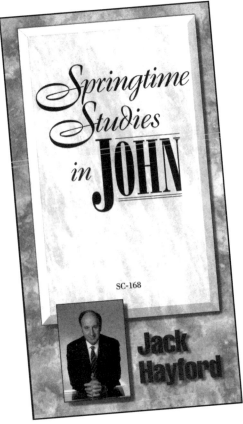

In this five-tape audio album, you will learn how to experience spiritual fruitfulness, as well as Spirit fullness.

SC168 $22.00

*An outline of the basic elements
in a growing life with Jesus.*

NEWBORN

This paperback book discusses the believer's relationship to God, how the Bible can help in one's spiritual journey, types of baptism, and the need for spending time with other believers.
NBN $4.99

Open to the fullness of the Spirit of Christ!

SPIRIT-FILLED
THE OVERFLOWING POWER OF THE HOLY SPIRIT

This book shows how to maintain wisdom and balance in daily Spirit-filled living. Its practical instruction on the Person and Power of the Spirit teaches the enablement and resources of spiritual gifts and graces.
SFL $4.99

*Want the Best Study Bible on the
Market Today?*

The
SPIRIT-FILLED LIFE BIBLE
may be what you're looking for!

The Spirit-Filled Life Bible is a powerful resource for enriching your relationship with Jesus Christ. Faith-filled, prophetic, and Spirit-empowered insights are featured in this one-of-a-kind study Bible. Here, in the light of God's Word, you will discover a Spirit-filled life rich in Godly characteristics. Available in English or Spanish.

Hardback Library Edition: reg. $37.99 **SFLHB** **$27.99**
*Call for availability and discounted prices
for genuine leather editions.*

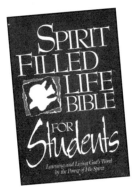

SPIRIT-FILLED LIFE BIBLE FOR STUDENTS

Help your favorite student learn and live God's Word by the Holy Spirit's power!

Softcover **SFLBS** **$15.99**

Unveil the Keys to Scripture!

HAYFORD'S BIBLE HANDBOOK

Hayford's Bible Handbook is an unparalleled resource that uniquely unveils the keys to Scripture, providing not only a wealth of information, but also a spiritual stimulus that will encourage your faith and service to Christ.

It unlocks Scripture with:

- Illuminating surveys of each book of the Bible.
- Helpful illustrations, time lines, maps, and charts.
- A complete Visual Survey of the Bible.
- An Encyclopedia Dictionary with over 1,300 entries that address subjects of particular interest to Spirit-filled believers.

This guide opens the riches of Scripture with a unique focus on practical ministry in the Holy Spirit's power—all to deepen your life in Christ. *reg. $24.99* **HBH $22.99**

This guide will open the riches of Scripture and deepen your life in Christ!

ORDER FORM

Qty.	Item	Code	Price	Total
____	_____	____	____	____
____	_____	____	____	____
____	_____	____	____	____
____	_____	____	____	____
____	_____	____	____	____
____	_____	____	____	____
____	_____	____	____	____
____	_____	____	____	____
____	_____	____	____	____
____	_____	____	____	____

Postage and Handling

$0.00 - $9.99 . . . . $2.95
$10.00 - $29.99 . . . . $4.95
$30.00 - $49.99 . . . . $6.95
$60.00 and up . . . . . . 15% of subtotal
(In the U.S.)
All orders outside the USA $8,
plus 20% of Subtotal

Subtotal _____

Add 8.25% sales tax to CA orders _____

Shipping and Handling _____

Donation (Optional) _____

Total _____

Name _____

Street Address _____

City _____ State _____ Zip _____

Phone Number (_____) _____

Method of Payment: ❏ Check or Money Order ❏ Visa ❏ MC

_____ / _____-_____-_____-_____ / _____
Signature   Card Number   Exp. Date

RESOURCES

LIVING · WAY
MINISTRIES

14820 Sherman Way, Van Nuys, CA 91405-2233

Please call for prices and ordering information:
1-800-776-8180 • 1-818-779-8480

Please include your remittance (U.S. currency only) with order.
Make check or money order payable to Living Way Ministries.